30 Days of Breath Prayers Found in the Psalms

With journal prompts for reflection and prayer.

By Kat Gibson

Phrases from Psalms 33-43 (some paraphrased).

© 2025 by Kat Gibson.

All rights reserved. No part of this may be reproduced in any form without written permission from Kat Gibson.

Scriptures taken from the Holy Bible, New International Version®, NIV®. Copyright © 1973, 1978, 1984, 2011 by Biblica, Inc.™ Used by permission of Zondervan. All rights reserved worldwide. www.zondervan.com The "NIV" and "New International Version" are trademarks registered in the United States Patent and Trademark Office by Biblica, Inc.™

Many of the Scripture verses used are my paraphrase, slightly shortened or, for example, changing 'His' (God's) to 'Your', to turn the verse into a prayer. This is not an interpretation or new translation; simply redaction where appropriate to allow for concise 'breath prayers'.

Cover design by Kat Gibson.

ISBN 9798312554830
Independently Published.

For all who long for God's gentle whisper
in the middle of the treadmill of each day.
May the presence of God be made known to us
in the moments when we least expect it.

Introduction

The 'Breath Prayer' is a wonderful way to slow down our frantic brains and calm our bodies for a few moments, bringing our attention to God and lingering there.

This practice has been written about by Christian contemplatives, monks and nuns and others throughout the centuries, and has become a solid feature of many people's daily walk with God. People pray words of the Bible, or other prayerful words, *slowly* and repetitively, in time with their breathing. Books have been written about it by a wide range of people, exploring the why and how and even the science behind its physical and psychological benefits (!) – but why don't we launch right in and try it out.

Practice a few of the 'breath prayers' on the next page – some of my favourites – to familiarise yourself with the process before starting your 30 Days. It's quite simple.

Slow down your breathing. Maybe thank God for being with you.

As you breathe in, say the first part in your mind.
As you breathe out, say the second part in your mind.
Repeat it for a couple of minutes, or longer if you'd like to.
Then be still and quiet for a few moments.
Perhaps God might want to say something to you.

Lord Jesus ... Have mercy.

(Or) *Lord Jesus Christ ... Have mercy on me, a sinner.*

Holy Father ... Thank You for Your love.

Your Kingdom come ... Your will be done.

Speak, Lord ... Your servant is listening.

Spirit of the living God ... Fall afresh on me.

Breath of God ... Breathe life.

Jesus ... I surrender.

You can use other words or phrases that come naturally to you in prayer or are meaningful to you – or use things that stand out to you from reading the Bible. Sometimes it is enough just to pray "Lord Jesus" as you breathe slowly.

In this little book we're using thirty beautiful phrases found spread out between ten of the Psalms – Psalms 33-43. There is space alongside each phrase for you to note down anything that comes to mind as you ponder the words, as well as the Breath Prayer itself. Don't analyse it with lots of intellectual thought, or pick it apart. This isn't a Bible Study, but a space for imagination, memory, tender curiosity, and maybe even the voice of God in the quiet.

Try to come back to your Breath Prayer at several moments throughout the day. Don't stress if you can't remember it; it's also good to just remember at various points throughout the day to pause, breathe slowly, and bring your attention to God.

Breathe in:
The word of the Lord is true;
Breathe out:
He is faithful in all he does.
(Psalm 33:4)

Take a few moments to ponder these words.

Note down any thoughts that come to mind.

What does it mean, to you, that God's word is true?

When have you experienced God's faithfulness in your life?

How does it feel, to know that He is *always* faithful?

At various moments throughout today, bring this verse to mind. Breathe deeply as you remember it, and use it as a prayer.

Breathe in:
The Lord spoke

Breathe out:
And it came to be.
(Psalm 33:9)

Take a few moments to ponder these words.

Note down any thoughts that come to mind.

What does it mean, to you, that God's voice made everything?

Have you ever heard God's voice? What did God say to you?

How does it feel, that the One who spoke Creation into being still speaks today, and wants to communicate with you?

At various moments throughout today, bring this verse to mind. Breathe deeply as you remember it, and use it as a prayer.

Breathe in:
The plans of the Lord
Breathe out:
Stand firm forever.
(Psalm 33:11)

Take a few moments to ponder these words.

Note down any thoughts that come to mind.

What does it mean, to you, that God's plans stand firm?

Do you know what plans God might have for your life?

What do you think about the plans God has for you?

How does it feel, to know that nothing can change God's plans?

At various moments throughout today, bring this verse to mind. Breathe deeply as you remember it, and use it as a prayer.

Breathe in:
We wait in hope for the Lord

Breathe out:
He is our help and our shield.

(Psalm 33:20)

Take a few moments to ponder these words.

Note down any thoughts that come to mind.

What does it mean, to you, to wait in hope for God?

When have you experienced God's help and protection?

How does it feel, to know that God is your help and your shield?

Where do you need God's help and protection this week?

At various moments throughout today, bring this verse to mind. Breathe deeply as you remember it, and use it as a prayer.

Breathe in:
In You our hearts rejoice
Breathe out:
For we trust in Your holy name.
(Psalm 33:21)

Take a few moments to ponder these words.

Note down any thoughts that come to mind.

What does it mean, to you, to trust in God's holy name?

What reasons do you have for your heart to rejoice in God?

What does *trusting* in God look like, in the middle of struggles?

What does *rejoicing* in God look like when life is really tough?

At various moments throughout today, bring this verse to mind. Breathe deeply as you remember it, and use it as a prayer.

Breathe in:
May Your unfailing love
Breathe out:
Rest upon us.
(Psalm 33:22)

Take a few moments to ponder these words.

Note down any thoughts that come to mind.

What does it mean, for God's unfailing love to rest on you?

Who do you know, who needs to experience God's love today?

What might life feel like if you were always aware of God's love?

At various moments throughout today, bring this verse to mind. Breathe deeply as you remember it, and use it as a prayer.

Breathe in:
We put our hope

Breathe out:
In You, O Lord.
(Psalm 33:22)

Take a few moments to ponder these words.

Note down any thoughts that come to mind.

If God were to ask what you hope for, how might you respond?

When have you consciously put your hope in God in the past?

What else might you be tempted to put your hope in?

What does it mean, to you, to really put your hope in God?

At various moments throughout today, bring this verse to mind. Breathe deeply as you remember it, and use it as a prayer.

Breathe in:
May Your praise

Breathe out:
Be always on my lips.
(Psalm 34:1)

Take a few moments to ponder these words.

Note down any thoughts that come to mind.

What does it mean, to you, that God loves when we praise him?

What reasons do you have to praise God?

What do you most want to thank God for?

How does it feel to praise God with your whole being?

At various moments throughout today, bring this verse to mind. Breathe deeply as you remember it, and use it as a prayer.

Breathe in:
The Lord has delivered me

Breathe out:
From all my fears.
(Psalm 34:4)

Take a few moments to ponder these words.

Note down any thoughts that come to mind.

What does it mean, to you, that God delivers you?

Have you experienced God's deliverance from fears in the past?

Are there current fears you need God to deliver you from?

How does it feel, to know and trust that God will deliver you?

At various moments throughout today, bring this verse to mind. Breathe deeply as you remember it, and use it as a prayer.

Breathe in:
Those who look to the Lord

Breathe out:
Are radiant.
(Psalm 34:5)

Take a few moments to ponder these words.

Note down any thoughts that come to mind.

What does it mean, to you, to 'look to the Lord'?

What does this verse bring to mind, for you?

What might it mean, for God to make you 'radiant'?

Who do you most want to see the radiance of God today?

At various moments throughout today, bring this verse to mind.
Breathe deeply as you remember it, and use it as a prayer.

Breathe in:
The whole earth is full
Breathe out:
Of Your unfailing love.
(Psalm 34:5)

Take a few moments to ponder these words.

Note down any thoughts that come to mind.

What does it mean, to you, that the earth is full of God's love?

What is it like to experience God's extravagant love?

How does it feel, to know that God's love is *unfailing*?

At various moments throughout today, bring this verse to mind. Breathe deeply as you remember it, and use it as a prayer.

Breathe in:
By the word of the Lord
Breathe out:
Were the heavens made.
(Psalm 34:6)

Take a few moments to ponder these words.

Note down any thoughts that come to mind.

What does it mean, to you, that God's word made the heavens?

How do you feel about God when you see a sunset or starry sky?

What might it mean for this same Word
to speak life and creativity into your situations today?

At various moments throughout today, bring this verse to mind.
Breathe deeply as you remember it, and use it as a prayer.

Breathe in:
Taste and see

Breathe out:
That the Lord is good.
(Psalm 34:8)

Take a few moments to ponder these words.

Note down any thoughts that come to mind.

What does it mean, to taste and see the Lord's goodness?

When have you tasted and seen God's goodness?

What does it mean, that in a world of brokenness, God is good?

How does it feel, to know in your heart that God is deeply good?

At various moments throughout today, bring this verse to mind.
Breathe deeply as you remember it, and use it as a prayer.

Breathe in:
Blessed are those

Breathe out:
Who take refuge in You.
(Psalm 34:8)

Take a few moments to ponder these words.

Note down any thoughts that come to mind.

What does it mean, to you, to 'take refuge' in God?

Why are those who take refuge in God blessed?

When have you taken refuge in God in the past?

How does it feel, to know that God is your refuge?

At various moments throughout today, bring this verse to mind. Breathe deeply as you remember it, and use it as a prayer.

Breathe in:
The Lord is close

Breathe out:
To the broken-hearted.
(Psalm 34:18)

Take a few moments to ponder these words.

Note down any thoughts that come to mind.

What does it mean, to you, that God is close to the broken-hearted?

What does closeness to God feel like, to you?

Have you experienced God's closeness in times of pain?

Do you know someone who deeply needs God's closeness?

At various moments throughout today, bring this verse to mind. Breathe deeply as you remember it, and use it as a prayer.

Breathe in:
Arise, O Lord

Breathe out:
And come to my aid.
(Psalm 35:2)

Take a few moments to ponder these words.

Note down any thoughts that come to mind.

What does it mean, to you, that God might come to your aid?

When have you cried out to God for help in the past?

Are there situations now where you really need God's help?

Who else are you desperate for God to help at this time?

At various moments throughout today, bring this verse to mind. Breathe deeply as you remember it, and use it as a prayer.

Breathe in:
O Lord, say to my soul,

Breathe out:
'I am your salvation'.
(Psalm 35:3)

Take a few moments to ponder these words.

Note down any thoughts that come to mind.

What does it mean, to you, that God is your salvation?

What have you been saved from? What is your salvation *for*?

Why might God remind your soul of His salvation today?

Who else do you long to experience God's salvation?

At various moments throughout today, bring this verse to mind. Breathe deeply as you remember it, and use it as a prayer.

Breathe in:
My whole being exclaims,

Breathe out:
'Who is like You, O Lord?'
(Psalm 35:10)

Take a few moments to ponder these words.

Note down any thoughts that come to mind.

What does it mean, to you, that God is absolutely unique?

When have you experienced awe and wonder at who God is?

What does it feel like to exclaim worship with your whole being?

At various moments throughout today, bring this verse to mind. Breathe deeply as you remember it, and use it as a prayer.

Breathe in:
Your love, O Lord

Breathe out:
Reaches to the heavens.
(Psalm 36:5)

Take a few moments to ponder these words.

Note down any thoughts that come to mind.

What does it mean, to you, that the Lord's love is *that* great?

What does it mean for your situations,
that God loves you that much?

What does it feel like to be loved so abundantly by God?

At various moments throughout today, bring this verse to mind.
Breathe deeply as you remember it, and use it as a prayer.

Breathe in:
How priceless, O Lord

Breathe out:
Is Your unfailing love.
(Psalm 36:7)

Take a few moments to ponder these words.

Note down any thoughts that come to mind.

What does it mean, to you, that the Lord's love is *priceless*?

What is God's extravagant and faithful love worth, to you?

What are the invitations of God's unfailing love to you today?

At various moments throughout today, bring this verse to mind. Breathe deeply as you remember it, and use it as a prayer.

Breathe in:
With You is the fountain of life

Breathe out:
In Your light we see light.
(Psalm 36:9)

Take a few moments to ponder these words.

Note down any thoughts that come to mind.

What does it mean, to you, that God has the 'fountain of life'?

What does God's light, and life, feel like, for you?

What might it mean for God to bring light
to every area of your life?

Who do you know who needs to see God's light today?

At various moments throughout today, bring this verse to mind.
Breathe deeply as you remember it, and use it as a prayer.

Breathe in:
You, Lord, are my stronghold
Breathe out:
In times of trouble.
(Psalm 37:39)

Take a few moments to ponder these words.

Note down any thoughts that come to mind.

What does it mean, to you, that God is your stronghold?

When have you known God as your stronghold in hardship?

How does it feel, to know that God will always be this for you?

Who do you know who needs to know God as their stronghold?

At various moments throughout today, bring this verse to mind.
Breathe deeply as you remember it, and use it as a prayer.

Breathe in:
The Lord set my feet on a rock

Breathe out:
And gave me a firm place to stand
(Psalm 40:2)

Take a few moments to ponder these words.

Note down any thoughts that come to mind.

What does this verse mean to you? Which words stand out?

When have you experienced God 'setting your feet on a rock'?

How does it feel, to be given 'a firm place to stand'?

Who do you know who needs that solidity this week?

At various moments throughout today, bring this verse to mind. Breathe deeply as you remember it, and use it as a prayer.

Breathe in:
Many, O Lord

Breathe out:
Are the wonders You have done.
(Psalm 40:5)

Take a few moments to ponder these words.

Note down any thoughts that come to mind.

What wonders have you experienced from God, in your life?

How does it feel, to have a sense of wonder at God's work?

What are you excited to praise God about, today?

At various moments throughout today, bring this verse to mind. Breathe deeply as you remember it, and use it as a prayer.

Breathe in:
O Lord, have mercy on me

Breathe out:
And heal me.
(Psalm 41:4)

Take a few moments to ponder these words.

Note down any thoughts that come to mind.

What does it mean, to you, to receive God's mercy?

When have you experienced God's mercy or healing in the past?

Where in your life do you need God's mercy, or healing, today?

At various moments throughout today, bring this verse to mind.
Breathe deeply as you remember it, and use it as a prayer.

Breathe in:
As the deer pants for water

Breathe out:
So my soul pants for You, O God.
(Psalm 42:1)

Take a few moments to ponder these words.

Note down any thoughts that come to mind.

What does it mean, to you, to deeply long for God like this?

When have you experienced such a longing for God?

What does that feel like, for you?

Are there areas of your life where you need God's living water?

At various moments throughout today, bring this verse to mind. Breathe deeply as you remember it, and use it as a prayer.

Breathe in:
By day the Lord directs his love

Breathe out:
At night his song is with me.
(Psalm 42:8)

Take a few moments to ponder these words.

Note down any thoughts that come to mind.

What does it mean, to you, that God is with you day and night?

When have you been most aware of God's presence with you?

What might it feel like to know God's 'song' with you at night?

What other image resonates, of God's presence with you?

At various moments throughout today, bring this verse to mind. Breathe deeply as you remember it, and use it as a prayer.

Breathe in:
Send Your light and Your truth

Breathe out:
Let them guide me.
(Psalm 43:3)

Take a few moments to ponder these words.

Note down any thoughts that come to mind.

What does it mean, to you, that God's light and truth can guide?

When have you known God's guidance in the past?

Who else do you know who deeply needs God's light and truth?

At various moments throughout today, bring this verse to mind. Breathe deeply as you remember it, and use it as a prayer.

Breathe in:
I will go to my God

Breathe out:
My joy and my delight.
(Psalm 43:4)

Take a few moments to ponder these words.

Note down any thoughts that come to mind.

What does this verse say to you? Which words most stand out?

What does it mean, to you, to 'go to God'?

When have you experienced God as your joy and delight?

How might God's joy and delight be present in your day, today?

At various moments throughout today, bring this verse to mind. Breathe deeply as you remember it, and use it as a prayer.

Breathe in:
Why are you downcast, my soul?

Breathe out:
Put your hope in God, my Saviour.
(Psalm 43:5)

Take a few moments to ponder these words.

Note down any thoughts that come to mind.

What does it mean, to you, to 'put your hope in God'?

When have you experienced God as Saviour when you've felt low?

Who do you know who needs God's hope and salvation?

At various moments throughout today, bring this verse to mind. Breathe deeply as you remember it, and use it as a prayer.

Which 'breath prayer' phrases most resonate with you?

Note them down, and carry them with you in your heart.

We believe that God longs for each of us to *thrive*.

We are called to become increasingly:
True to who we are designed to be,
Hopeful about life and the future,
In healthy **Relationship** with God and with others,
Invested in our own wellbeing and growth,
Aware of our **Value** as unique and beloved individuals,
and **Empathic** towards others, even amid differences.

Our hope is that this prayer resource might contribute to this in some small way. We pray that you who read and respond to these words might be led by God to increasingly *thrive*.

If anything in this little book particularly strikes you, blesses you, challenges you or upsets you, and you'd like to talk with me about it, please do get in touch. Please also let me know if you'd like to use this resource with your church, small-group, retreat or class. Email: katgibson.thrive@gmail.com

Printed in Great Britain
by Amazon